1 Page
AT A TIME

A DAILY creative COMPANION

ADAM J. KURTZ
(STILL JUST SOME GUY)

A TarcherPerigee Book

tarcherperigee

AN IMPRINT OF PENGUIN RANDOM HOUSE LLC

COPYRIGHT © 2014 BY ADAM J. KURTZ

Tarcher and Perigee are registered trademarks, and the colophon is a trademark of Penguin Random House LLC.

Most TarcherPerigee books are available at special quantity discounts for bulk purchase for sales promotions, premiums, fund-raising, and educational needs. Special books or book excerpts also can be created to fit specific needs. For details, write: SpecialMarkets@penguinrandomhouse.com.

ISBN: 978-0-14-312988-2
PROPRIETARY ISBN: 978-1-101-94956-6

Printed in the United States of America

4th Printing

IN MEMORY OF
Blanche Davids Gewirtz
WHO TAUGHT ME TO:

1. *never* BE AFRAID TO ASK
2. HAVE A *little* SUGAR
3. APPRECIATE LIFE'S *surprises*
4. DOCUMENT *everything*

"I LOVE YOU, A BUSHEL & A PECK"

THIS COULD BE
anything:

- ☐ A JOURNAL
- ☐ A KEEPSAKE
- ☐ A CALENDAR
- ☐ A FRIEND
- ☑ ALL OF THE ABOVE

THE *rest* IS
UP TO

YOU!

(WITH A LITTLE HELP)

YOU HAVE
everything
YOU NEED

WHAT ARE YOUR GOALS FOR
THE NEXT YEAR? WRITE BELOW.

PEOPLE I CAN ALWAYS CALL

Marilyn Andrejko
BEST FRIEND

No one
HAS A CAR

Nicole Ano (mom?
A PARENT

Sophie
ALWAYS READY TO PARTY

Hunter thompson
COOL SIBLING

Marilyn
KNOWS EVERYTHING

No one
LESS COOL SIBLING

Ava
KNOWS JUST ENOUGH

Aunt cary
FAVORITE AUNT

NaNa
GRANDPARENT

Ava
OWES ME A FAVOR

Natalia
1 MORE

SELECT THE FEELINGS
THAT RESONATE MOST

- ☐ WOW I AM SO HAPPY TO BE ALIVE
- ☐ I JUST NEED TO KEEP AT IT
- ☑ ANYTHING IS POSSIBLE
- ☑ LOVE IS STUPID (BUT CAN I PLS)
- ☐ I AM AFRAID OF DEATH, BUT APPRECIATE THAT IT IS INEVITABLE
- ☑ I CARE ABOUT OTHERS MORE THAN MYSELF
- ☑ THE INTERNET IS OVERWHELMING, BUT I CAN'T STOP
- ☐ BE THE CHANGE YOU WANT TO... WHATEVER
- ☑ PEOPLE CAN CHANGE (THEMSELVES), EVEN ME
- ☑ IF I CAN MAKE IT THROUGH THIS, I CAN MAKE IT THROUGH ANYTHING
- ☐ I HAVE MY "1 THING" THAT WILL ALWAYS KEEP ME GOING
- ☐ WOW THIS BOOK IS KIND OF INTENSE

WHAT TIME IS IT?

Some pages are just about you, no prompt, no jokes.
Don't be afraid! Don't even think, just write or draw, just let it happen!

LEARN TO DRAW

STEP 1.
DRAW TWO SQUARES BELOW

CONGRATULATIONS, YOU DID IT!

GO OUT OF YOUR WAY TO DO SOMETHING
YOU'VE NEVER DONE BEFORE.

TAPE A BUSINESS
CARD TO THIS PAGE:

Jackdishaw

" wannadate "

WHOSE IS IT?
WHERE IS IT FROM?

*IF AT FIRST YOU DON'T SUCCEED, THAT'S OK. IF YOU NEVER SUCCEED, I DON'T KNOW WHAT TO TELL YOU, HONESTLY.

HEY!
WHAT
HAVE YOU
BEEN UP TO
LATELY?

DESCRIBE A CHILDHOOD BIRTHDAY

FREE SPACE

* You'll see these wide open spaces as you move along.
Sometimes there's just no clear direction. Take a deep breath and try to enjoy it.

WHAT ARE YOU UP TO?
[📷 SHARE] THIS PAGE WITH #JK1PAGE
SO WE CAN TAKE A LOOK!

WHAT'S YOUR NAME?
WHY WERE YOU NAMED
  THIS & WHO DECIDED?
WHAT DOES IT MEAN?
WHAT ABOUT NICKNAMES?

If you find numbers overwhelming, a grid can help. Space them out and add them up! It's not so bad if you just think about it differently. Draw your first grid here. ✱

THINK OF SOMETHING
YOU'RE INSECURE ABOUT,
THEN WRITE IT HUGE.
FILL THE ENTIRE SPACE!
STARE AT IT. NOW TURN
THE PAGE.

WHERE DO YOU THINK YOU'LL BE IN 5 YEARS?
ARE YOU "ON TRACK" OR NOT? ARE YOU
FAIRLY SURE OR GUESSING? IS THIS QUESTION
JUST REALLY SCARY & AWFUL?

COPY THE LINE 20 TIMES,
OR UNTIL YOU LEARN YOUR LESSON!

I CAN DO ANYTHING

DESCRIBE SOMETHING YOU SAW ON THE GROUND TODAY

(WHERE WAS IT? WHO PUT IT THERE?)

SEND A TEXT TO THAT NEW
PERSON YOU MET LAST NIGHT.
(DON'T BE NERVOUS!)

GO OFF
THE GRID!

FILL OUT YOUR
SICK DAY CHECKLIST:

- ☐ LOTS OF DRINKS
- ☐ TISSUES
- ☐ VITAMIN C
- ☐ A LITTLE SYMPATHY
- ☐
- ☐
- ☐
- ☐
- ☐
- ☐
- ☐

DEAR MOM,

WRITE A LETTER TO YOUR MOM

WRITE YOURSELF A
SECRET MOTIVATION,
THEN FOLD THIS
PAGE UP TIGHT!

✱ Hmm, that last folded page looks pretty interesting... QUICK, FILL THIS WITH A DISTRACTION!

DESCRIBE YOURSELF IN
15 WORDS, AS A
SENTENCE OR A LIST.

EVERYTHING THAT WENT WRONG TODAY:

NEVER FORGET:
YOU'RE LITERALLY A
GIANT TOOL. LAUGH ABOUT
BEING A TOOL & REMEMBER
THAT EVERYONE ELSE
IS 1 TOO.

CARE PACKAGE

FILL THIS BOX WITH LOTS OF GOOD STUFF!

1
BANANA

* You know what else would be good? An "I don't care" package... 1 big box full of "LEAVE ME ALONE."

RETURN TO SENDER

GET POSTAL ADDRESSES FOR 3 FAR-AWAY FRIENDS & WRITE THEM POSTCARDS THIS YEAR. COME BACK TO CHECK THEM OFF WHEN YOU DO!

DESCRIBE HOW YOU MET YOUR BEST FRIEND

*
Are you BFF4EVER? Pinky promise?

TAPE A RESTAURANT CHECK TO THIS PAGE & DESCRIBE YOUR MEAL

WHAT I _REALLY_ WANTED TO SAY:

...and now, *WHAT I REALLY REALLY WANTED TO SAY BUT DIDN'T EVEN WANT TO WRITE DOWN BUT NOW MY BOOK IS MAKING ME DO IT SO HERE GOES NOTHING:* ✳

WHAT WAS THE MOST CHALLENGING
THING YOU DEALT WITH LAST YEAR?

CREATE YOUR OWN CONVERSATION HEARTS!

H8 U

Sorry not sorry

have fun!!!

FINE!

Okay

KEEP GOING!

COVER THIS PAGE IN POP-UP ADS! ✗

IT'S JUST

PAPER!

QUIETLY DO GOOD FOR OTHERS.
GIVE TO SOMEONE ON THE STREET,
LEAVE AN EXTRA-LARGE TIP.
DON'T TELL ANYONE. NO EGO BOOST.
JUST NOTE THE DATE BELOW.

THERE IS NO EXCUSE, BUT

✱ Draw a grid, then fill boxes with big X marks to make your own cross-stitch pattern.

WHAT IS YOUR GREATEST
WISH FOR THE FUTURE?

TAKE A MOMENT TO
OBSERVE SOMETHING
SMALL TODAY. WHAT
DID YOU SEE?

MAKE A PLAYLIST FOR A BIRTHDAY PARTY:

1. THE GRATES
   "19 20 20"

2.

3.

4.

5.

6.

7.

8.

WAIT, DON'T POST THAT! WRITE YOUR ANGRY STATUS UPDATE BELOW, THEN 📷 SHARE A PHOTO... IF YOU EVEN WANT TO ANYMORE.

ARE WE THERE YET?

☑ NO   ☑ NO   ☑ NO

☑ NO   ☑ NO   ☑ NO

☑ NO   ☑ NO   ☑ NO

☑ NO   ☑ NO   ☑ NO

☑ NO   ☑ NO   ☑ NO

☑ NO   ☑ NO   ☑ NO

☑ NO   ☑ NO   ☑ NO

☑ NO   ☑ NO   ☑ NO

☑ NO   ☑ NO   ☐ YES

*treat yourself to a nap!

♡ I LIKED THIS
♡ I LIKED THIS
♡ I LIKED THIS   ♡ I LIKED THIS
♡ I LIKED THIS   ♡ I LIKED THIS
♡ I LIKED THIS ♡ I LIKED THIS

TAKE A DEEP BREATH
& COUNT TO 10, REPEAT

~~||||~~ ~~||||~~

Breathing seems so obvious, but don't you feel better after all those deep breaths? Take one more, really inhale deeply through your nose, and feel your chest rise. Hold it for a few seconds, then let it out super slowly. O-K, let's keep going. ✳

YOU CAN DO IT!
(DEPENDING ON
WHAT IT IS)

DRAW YOURSELF AN
IDENTIFICATION CARD.
WHAT'S ON IT? WHAT
MATTERS?

AGE? HEIGHT?
ARE YOU SMILING FOR
THE PHOTO OR NOT?

DREAM JOBS:

~~NAP TAKER~~ ~~CANDY EATER~~

IT'S JUST PAPER! CAREFULLY CUT THIS PAGE INTO A SINGLE LONG RIBBON. OR DON'T!

CONNECT THE DOTS IN ANY ORDER:

WHAT DO YOU SEE?

* Draw your own random dots and try that one again!

LIST 5 FRIENDS YOU THINK YOU'LL HAVE FOREVER:

1 _____

2 _____

3 _____

4 _____

5 _____

TAPE A BUS, TRAIN,
OR PLANE TICKET
TO THIS PAGE:
(WHERE ARE YOU GOING? WHY?)

HOW I AM FEELING

- ☐ EVERYTHING SUCKS
- ☐ SOME THINGS SUCK
- ☐ SOMETIMES I SUCK
- ☐ SOMETIMES EVERYONE ELSE SUCKS
- ☐ NOTHING EVER SUCKS!
- ☐ EVERYTHING SUCKS SOMETIMES
- ☐ SUCK IT

 SHARE #JK1PAGE

I like jack

HEY!
WHAT
ARE YOU
UP TO
TODAY?

party

COMPLETE THIS STATEMENT UNTIL
THE PAGE IS FULL:

IF I CAN DO <u>this</u>, I CAN DO ANYTHING.

ENJOY THE UNKNOWN

TAPE A SMALL
PHOTO OR IMAGE
HERE, THEN TRY
TO COPY IT BELOW!

WHEN LIFE CLOSES A DOOR,
IT OPENS A WINDOW. BUT
IF THE DOOR ISN'T LOCKED,
THERE'S NO REASON YOU
CAN'T JUST OPEN IT FOR
YOURSELF, RIGHT?

WRITE IT HUGE

These big pages are the best! You can't always scream in public but you can definitely shout in here. ✳

✳ Draw yourself a grid. Can you fit a tiny word in each box? Can you write a story that fits perfectly?

DRAW YOUR DREAM HOUSE
(OR APARTMENT! OR CASTLE!)

IT'S JUST PAPER!
DRAW SOME SALT, THEN
THROW IT OVER YOUR
SHOULDER FOR LUCK.

PAUSE AT AN OVERPASS
& COUNT THE CARS ZOOMING
BELOW. HOW DOES IT FEEL?

MAKE A PLAYLIST TO GO FOR A RUN:

1. WEEKENDS
   "RAINGIRLS"

2.

3.

4.

5.

6.

7.

8.

TRAVEL PLANS: WHAT LANDMARK DO YOU MOST WANT TO SEE?

SNACKS TO EAT

- ☐ PRETZELS
- ☐ ICE CREAM
- ☐ DONUT
- ☐ ANOTHER DONUT
- ☐ LICORICE
- ☐ CANDY BAR
- ☐ CHIPS
- ☐ CHIPS & DIP
- ☐ ~~CARROT STICKS~~
- ☐ BIRTHDAY CAKE
- ☐ JELLY BEANS
- ☐ 3 COOKIES
- ☐ 1 MORE DONUT
- ☐ GUMMY WORMS

PRESERVE SOME FEELINGS IN THE JARS.
DRAW SOME MORE JARS. YOU'LL BE ABLE
TO ENJOY THEM IN COLDER MONTHS!

WRITE A PEP TALK FOR A BAD DAY.
(WHAT DO YOU DO WHEN LIFE GIVES YOU LEMONS?)

I usually like to cry and be in bed
watchling tiktoks

DO YOU BELIEVE IN SOULMATES?
IS YOURS OUT THERE? DO WE GET
MULTIPLE OPTIONS? WRITE A
NOTE TO YOURS, WHEREVER THEY ARE!

WRITE DOWN EVERYTHING
THAT'S BOTHERING YOU,
THEN JUST TURN THE PAGE

QUARTERLY CHECK-IN

THINK ABOUT THE LAST 3 MONTHS
& RANK YOURSELF ON THE SMILEY SCALE.

LET'S
FACE IT ➔ ☺   ☻   ☹
        GOOD   FAIR   POOR

GENERAL OUTLOOK ◯	PERSONAL GROWTH ◯	PHYSICAL HEALTH ◯
PLANNING AHEAD ◯	TAKING CARE ◯	EATING WELL ◯
SLEEPING HABITS ◯	BEING AWESOME ◯	MENTAL HEALTH ◯
SOME DAILY CREATIVITY ◯	SHOWING KINDNESS ◯	CALLING HOME ◯
WORKING HARD ◯	HAVING FUN ◯	BEING A FRIEND ◯
STAYING CALM ◯	TRYING HARD ◯	ENJOYING YOUR SPACE ◯
EARNING A LIVING ◯	GOING OUTDOORS ◯	THAT 1 THING ◯
FEELING CONTENT ◯	FUNNY TWEETS ◯	FIGURING IT OUT ◯

SIT DOWN IN THE
SHOWER. THAT'S IT.

FUTURE PET NAMES:

* NO MATTER WHAT, THERE WILL ALWAYS BE PIZZA.

WRITE AN INSPIRATIONAL QUOTE BELOW, THEN SHARE IT ONLINE WITH YOUR FRIENDS!

 #JK1PAGE

DRAW A LAYER CAKE
& DESCRIBE EACH LAYER

*
That's a huge cake! Maybe we should draw a salad next, or at least a celery stick or something.

GIVE THIS PAGE TO A FRIEND

WRITE THAT THING YOU PROMISED NOT TO JOKE ABOUT ANYMORE THAT IS STILL TOTALLY FUNNY.

TAPE A $5 BILL

TO THIS PAGE & FORGET ABOUT IT!

WRITE A LETTER TO YOURSELF
SIX MONTHS FROM NOW

Cool, now write a letter to yourself three minutes from now!

✳

LIST EVERYTHING YOU CAN
REMEMBER BEING AFRAID OF,
THEN CROSS OUT STUFF YOU'VE
GOTTEN OVER!

SPIDERS

~~TEENAGERS~~

~~THE DARK~~

MUMMIES

THERE IS NOTHING IN YOUR WAY

WEAR SOMETHING
INSIDE-OUT TODAY,
& TELL ME HOW
IT WENT:

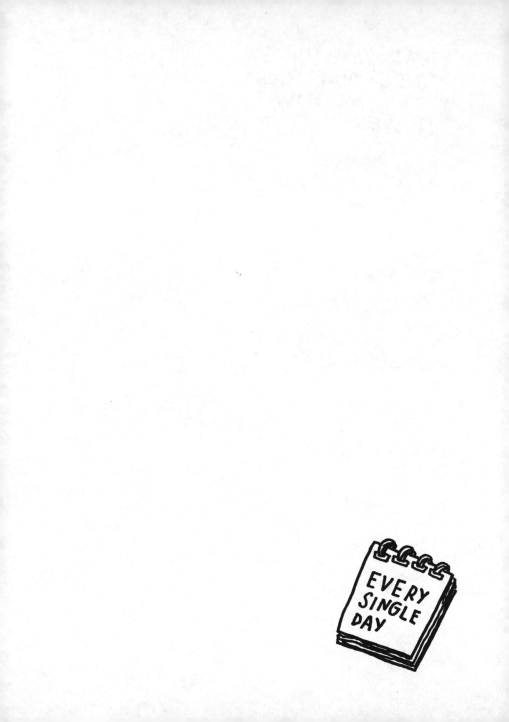

I didn't want to say anything but you've been pressing really hard with that pen. Can you just chill out please? ✳

FILL ALL OF THIS SPACE.
STARE AT IT.
NOW TURN THE PAGE.

IS HAPPINESS EVEN A PLACE?
DO YOU EVER JUST "GET THERE,"
OR IS IT MORE AN OUTLOOK ON
LIFE & ITS PROGRESS?

JUST WRITE YOUR NAME.
JUST BE HERE RIGHT NOW.
THAT'S IT.

TAKE YOURSELF FOR A
COFFEE OR TEA.
SIT OUTSIDE. DESCRIBE
3 PEOPLE YOU SAW.

WATER YOU

WAITING FOR?

SEEMS LIKE
* NOBODY NOTICED,
DON'T WORRY
ABOUT IT!

TO—DO LIST:

- ☐ MAKE A LIST
- ☐ CHECK FIRST 2 BOXES

treat yourself to *a movie!*

STAND IN PLACE FOR 1 MINUTE.
CLOSE YOUR EYES & BREATHE IN
& OUT VERY SLOWLY. FOCUS ON
THE SIZE OF YOUR BODY IN RELATION
TO THE SPACE. NO, LIKE OUTER
SPACE. MEOW LIKE A DOG. ARF!
POPCORN. HORSESHOE. WHAT'S
HAPPENING RIGHT NOW? OKAY,
NOW OPEN YOUR EYES.

DRAW BANANAS FOR 20 MINUTES,
THEN SPLIT!

TAPE A PAGE FROM ANOTHER BOOK
OR NOTEBOOK TO THIS PAGE
(I GET LONELY SOMETIMES)

YOU'RE _A_ _STAR!_ PROBABLY.
WHAT WOULD A FILM OF
YOUR LIFE BE CALLED?
WHO WOULD PLAY YOU?
DRAW A POSTER FOR IT!

EIGHT BEST PIZZA SLICES

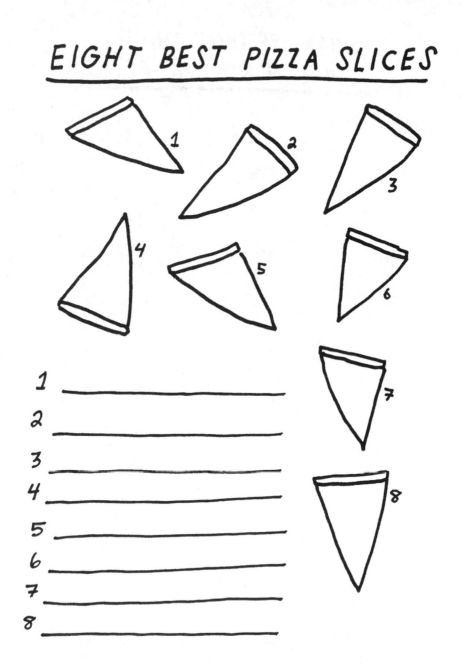

1 _____
2 _____
3 _____
4 _____
5 _____
6 _____
7 _____
8 _____

WHAT ARE SOME THINGS YOU CAN BUY FOR $1?

WHAT ARE SOME THINGS YOU CAN'T BUY AT ALL?

✳ Have you ever been thrown a surprise party? Tell me all about it, I'm jealous!

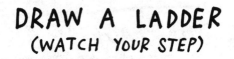

DRAW A LADDER
(WATCH YOUR STEP)

WRITE A NOTE TO
YOUR FUTURE SELVES.

WHAT DID YOU WANT TO
BE "WHEN YOU GREW UP?"
HOW DO YOU FEEL NOW?

```
┌─────────────────────────────────────────┬──┐
│ NEW MESSAGE                              │ ─│
├─────────────────────────────────────────┴──┤
│ TO: YOU                                     │
│ CC: EVERYONE ELSE                           │
│ BCC: ME                                     │
├─────────────────────────────────────────────┤
│ SUBJECT:                                    │
├─────────────────────────────────────────────┤
│                                             │
│                                             │
│                                             │
│                                             │
│                                             │
│                                             │
│                                             │
│                                             │
│                                             │
│                                             │
└─────────────────────────────────────────────┘
```

WRITE AN EMAIL TO ANYONE
WHO EVER DOUBTED YOU...
INCLUDING YOURSELF!

Have you ever written an email and then just saved it without sending? Sometimes just writing is all you need. Use this page to get something down on paper that you just need to take out of your brain. ✱

TAPE SOMETHING SHINY
TO THIS PAGE. WHAT
IS IT FROM?

MAKE SPACE FOR YOURSELF

YOU COULD DO THIS
WITH YOUR
EYES CLOSED!

RT AFTER ME:
I CAN DO ANYTHING
#JK1PAGE

110 TWEET

GIVE THIS PAGE TO A FRIEND

DON'T DO ANYTHING.
SIT & TALK FOR HOURS.
THIS IS THE BEST PART
OF BEING FRIENDS.

Draw a grid. Or do whatever you want! Embrace the structure or fight the system. Make your own rules! YEAHHH! ✳

EVERY ROMANTIC RELATIONSHIP
TEACHES US ABOUT SOMETHING WE
WANT OR NEED IN A PARTNER.
WHAT HAVE YOU LEARNED SO FAR?

Shhh…

DRAW AN ODDLY-SPECIFIC
"DO NOT DISTURB" SIGN

SIT IN ONE PLACE FOR
TEN MINUTES & DRAW
WHAT YOU OBSERVE.

MAKE A PLAYLIST FOR GETTING EVEN:

1. MICHELLE BRANCH
   "ARE YOU HAPPY NOW?"

2.

3.

4.

5.

6.

7.

8.

TRAVEL PLANS: PLAN A WEEKEND GETAWAY (& GO!)

INTERNET TO-DO LIST

- ☐ CHECK EMAIL
- ☐ CHECK NOTIFICATIONS
- ☐ UPDATE STATUS
- ☐ SEARCH NEWS ITEM
- ☐ TWEET
- ☐ READ FAVORITE BLOG
- ☐ CHECK EMAIL
- ☐ BROWSE ONLINE SHOP
- ☐ READ FRIEND'S BLOG
- ☐ UPDATE STATUS ABOUT IT
- ☐ SEARCH FOR YOURSELF
- ☐ PLAY A GAME
- ☐ WATCH A VIDEO
- ☐ TWICE
- ☐ OMG
- ☐ CHECK EMAIL AGAIN
- ☐ CHAT YOUR MOM
- ☐ SIGN OFF
- ☐ PULL OUT PHONE

*treat *yourself to *a day* off!
*   *   *   *

*
HELLO? IS ANYONE THERE? WORDS? DOODLES? WHERE ARE YOU GUYS? HELLO? WHAT IS HAPPENING TO ME?!

WHO IS THE 1 PERSON
YOU CAN ALWAYS COUNT
ON? WRITE DOWN THEIR
PHONE NUMBER. ADDRESS.
EMAIL. BIRTHDAY. DO NOT
LET THIS PERSON GO.
TELL THEM WHAT THEY
MEAN TO YOU.

IT'S JUST PAPER!
TEAR THIS PAGE IN
HALF.

You're tearing this one in half, right? *

THINGS MIGHT NOT BE OK
TODAY OR TOMORROW, BUT
WE'LL MAKE IT, 1 PAGE AT
A TIME, SO HANG IN THERE!

CLICK TO CONTINUE

www.MYSELF.COM

ABOUT ME:

WHO I'D LIKE TO MEET:

SHARE #JK1PAGE

10 THINGS I AM REALLY GOOD AT:

1. MAKING LISTS
2.
3.
4.
5.
6.
7.
8.
9.
10.

*DON'T FORGET THAT TOMORROW
IS LITERALLY JUST 1 DAY AWAY.

WRITE SOME <u>TERRIBLE</u> ADVICE, THEN PRACTICE IGNORING IT.

Have you noticed that I have like a massive sweet tooth? Do you have any candy? ✳

he is dating
someone.....

SNAP OUT
OF IT!

its Not
me <|3

WHAT ARE YOU EXCITED FOR?

THIS BOOK ⇄ 32 PAGES AGO

DRAW A LADDER
(WATCH YOUR STEP)

TAPE A PARAGRAPH FROM
A NEWSPAPER TO THIS PAGE.
CROSS OUT ANY PARTS YOU
DON'T LIKE.

WRITE A LETTER TO A
7-YEAR-OLD. CHOOSE
YOUR WORDS CAREFULLY!

SIT AT AN AIRPORT,
TRAIN STATION OR
BUS STOP. WATCH
PEOPLE COME & GO.
WHERE ARE THEY HEADED?

HEY MAN,
WHAT'S
GOING
ON?

HAVING A ROUGH DAY?
YOU'RE PROBABLY NOT THE ONLY 1.
[📷 SHARE] A HAPPY THOUGHT
WITH #JK1PAGE, &
CHEER US ALL UP!

THIS COULD BE ANYTHING

Whenever you feel like nobody understands you, remember that it's probably because you're like really weird. Then flap your giant wings and fly off into the sunset. Land on the mountain near your cave. Breathe fire into the sky, then settle down to watch your eggs. WAIT, ARE YOU A DRAGON? That. Is. Awesome.

✳

WRITE SOMETHING IN ALL
CAPS & THEN PRESS

REPLY ALL

GIVE THIS PAGE TO A FRIEND

WRITE ABOUT A FAVORITE
MEMORY OR EXPERIENCE
YOU HAD TOGETHER.

LEAVE TINY ENCOURAGING NOTES IN DIFFERENT PUBLIC SPACES

YOU'RE DOING IT RIGHT, HONESTLY. GO YOU!

THIS MIGHT BE WHAT YOU WERE WAITING FOR.

TODAY IS THE DAY YOU FINALLY TREAT YOURSELF!

THIS FEELS LIKE THE START OF SOMETHING GOOD!

@CUTIE82_ASPX3   21h
WOW UR CRAZY OMG IS THIS
YOU IN THE VIDEO??
blt.ly/xp94a6zzQ

💬 VIEW ← REPLY ★FAV ··· MORE

COPY THE LINE 20 TIMES,
OR UNTIL YOU LEARN YOUR LESSON!

I AM VERY RETWEETABLE

IGNORE THE HATERS
(SERIOUSLY, LEAVE THAT BLANK!)

IT'S JUST PAPER!
WRITE A NOTE ON A DOLLAR
BILL & TAPE IT TO THIS PAGE.

WHAT IS IT "WORTH" NOW?

CHECK OFF THE HOURS AS THEY GO BY:

☐ 12 AM   ☐ 12 PM
☐ 1 AM   ☐ 1 PM
☐ 2 AM   ☐ 2 PM
☐ 3 AM   ☐ 3 PM
☐ 4 AM   ☐ 4 PM
☐ 5 AM   ☐ 5 PM
☐ 6 AM   ☐ 6 PM
☐ 7 AM   ☐ 7 PM
☐ 8 AM   ☐ 8 PM
☐ 9 AM   ☐ 9 PM
☐ 10 AM   ☐ 10 PM
☐ 11 AM   ☐ 11 PM

O-K, IT'S TOMORROW!

MOST OF THE TIME
WE KNOW EXACTLY
WHAT WE NEED TO HEAR.

SO WHAT'S GOING ON?
WRITE DOWN THE FACTS,
THEN FACE THEM!

*

Have you ever gotten a professional massage? It is actually one of the best things ever.
Save it for when you're really overworked....your body has earned it, promise!

DRAW A FAMILY PORTRAIT!

* YOU CAN DO IT (PROBABLY)

QUARTERLY CHECK-IN

THINK ABOUT THE LAST 3 MONTHS
& RANK YOURSELF ON THE SMILEY SCALE.

LET'S
FACE IT >   ☺   ☹
            GOOD   FAIR   POOR

GENERAL OUTLOOK ○	PERSONAL GROWTH ○	PHYSICAL HEALTH ○
PLANNING AHEAD ○	TAKING CARE ○	EATING WELL ○
SLEEPING HABITS ○	BEING AWESOME ○	MENTAL HEALTH ○
SOME DAILY CREATIVITY ○	SHOWING KINDNESS ○	CALLING HOME ○
WORKING HARD ○	HAVING FUN ○	BEING A FRIEND ○
STAYING CALM ○	TRYING HARD ○	ENJOYING YOUR SPACE ○
EARNING A LIVING ○	GOING OUTDOORS ○	THAT 1 THING ○
FEELING CONTENT ○	FUNNY TWEETS ○	FIGURING IT OUT ○

TODAY
NEARLY
KILLED ME
BUT I'M
O-K

YOU CAN LIVE FOREVER,
BUT IN CASE YOU DON'T,
WHAT WILL YOUR
TOMBSTONE SAY?

LIST <u>5</u> PLACES THAT YOU WOULD RATHER BE RIGHT NOW:

1 _____

2 _____

3 _____

4 _____

5 _____

& WHY?

IT'S JUST PAPER!
WHO CARES, DUDE.

BUILD THE PERFECT SANDWICH

BREAD

LABEL
THE
REST

BREAD

(CRUMBS ARE A PART OF LIFE.
THE SANDWICH IS STILL PERFECT!)

DRAW YOURSELF A TROPHY OR OTHER LARGE AWARD.

WOW, THAT'S BIG, YOU MUST BE REALLY IMPORTANT!

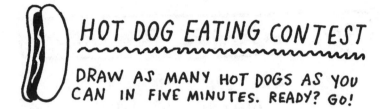

HOT DOG EATING CONTEST

DRAW AS MANY HOT DOGS AS YOU
CAN IN FIVE MINUTES. READY? GO!

GIVE THIS PAGE TO A FRIEND

WHY ARE WE FRIENDS?
WHAT MAKES US SO
AWESOME TOGETHER?
(BE CHEESY, IT'S OK!)

TAPE A PHOTO YOU
LOVE TO THIS PAGE.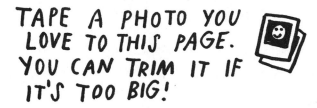
YOU CAN TRIM IT IF
IT'S TOO BIG!

GO BACK TO A PAGE YOU LEFT
BLANK BEFORE & TRY AGAIN!

GIVE ME A HIGH-FIVE, PAT YOURSELF ON THE BACK,
WAVE TO A FRIEND, OR DRAW YOUR HAND IN MINE.

TAPE A LOOP OF THREAD
TO THIS PAGE SO YOU
   NEVER FORGET THAT
1 THING.

HEY,
ARE
YOU
FEELING
OKAY?

1. DRAW A BEAUTIFUL FRAME
2. PUT NOTHING IN IT
3. GOOD JOB

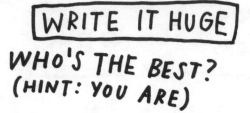

WHO'S THE BEST?
(HINT: YOU ARE)

ADMIT
IT

04893

WHAT ARE YOUR GOALS
FOR THE REST OF THE YEAR?

COPY THE LINE 20 TIMES,
OR UNTIL YOU LEARN YOUR LESSON!

I WILL DO THAT THING

GIVE THIS PAGE TO A STRANGER

IS THIS AWKWARD? DON'T WORRY, IT'S "FOR ART."
IT'S MY FAULT, I'M A VERY PUSHY JOURNAL.

DRAW A QUICK DOODLE OF THE PERSON WHO HANDED YOU THIS.

MAKE A PLAYLIST OF AWESOME COVER SONGS:

1. WHEN SAINTS Go MACHINE
"BITTERSWEET SYMPHONY"

2.

3.

4.

5.

6.

7.

8.

HOW-TO: DRAW A RECTANGLE

1. TRY TO DRAW A SQUARE
2. GOOD JOB!

FEELINGS I FELT

- ☐ SAD
- ☐ MAD
- ☐ GLAD
- ☐ NICE
- ☐ NOT NICE
- ☐ JEALOUS
- ☐ PROUD
- ☐ GRUMPY
- ☐ JOYFUL
- ☐ STRESSED
- ☐ TIRED
- ☐ BORED
- ☐ APATHETIC
- ☐ PATHETIC
- ☐ HAPPY
- ☐ FRANTIC
- ☐ SLOW
- ☐ VERY SLOW
- ☐ LOVE
- ☐ SURE

treat yourself *to that* *thing!* *

```
┌────────────────────────────────────────┬──┐
│ NEW MESSAGE                             │▬ │
├────────────────────────────────────────┴──┤
│ TO:                                        │
│ CC:                                        │
│ BCC:                                       │
├────────────────────────────────────────────┤
│ SUBJECT:                                   │
├────────────────────────────────────────────┤
│                                            │
│                                            │
│                                            │
│                                            │
│                                            │
│                                            │
│                                            │
│                                            │
│                                            │
│                                            │
└────────────────────────────────────────────┘
```

TAKE A PERSONAL DAY!
EMAIL AN EXCUSE TO YOUR BOSS.

WRITE SOMETHING #WORTHWHILE,
THEN #RUIN IT WITH #HASHTAGS.

IT'S JUST PAPER!
CUT THIS INTO STRIPS
& MAKE A CHAIN.

If you draw patterns on this side, your paper chains will be much more exciting! Maybe something to cover up my annoying sentence. Why would I even put this here? *

HOW DO I M

SEARCH

HOW DO I MAKE TOAST?
HOW DO I MAKE A JOKE?
HOW DO I MEET ALIENS?
HOW DO I MEET COOL GUYS?
HOW DO I MOVE THIS ROCK?

IF A SANDWICH WAS NAMED
AFTER YOU, WHAT WOULD IT
BE CALLED? WHAT WOULD
BE IN IT? WHY ARE YOU
RECEIVING SUCH AN HONOR?

$5.99

SPECIAL

LIST <u>10</u> THINGS THAT MAKE YOU HAPPY:

1 _____

2 _____

3 _____

4 _____

5 _____

6 _____

7 _____

8 _____

9 _____

10 _____

* I AM JUST A BOOK, BUT
I BELIEVE IN YOU

DESCRIBE YOUR DREAM DATE

~~A 10 HOUR NAP, ALONE~~
~~FREE WIFI~~

✱ Why am I so tired today?

COMFORT ZONE:

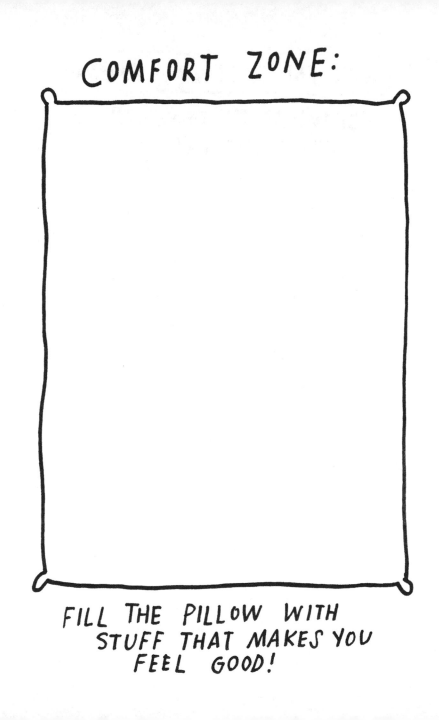

FILL THE PILLOW WITH
STUFF THAT MAKES YOU
FEEL GOOD!

GIVE THIS PAGE TO A FRIEND

DRAW US IN 30 YEARS
(SHOW NO MERCY!)

TAPE A SMALL LEAF TO THIS PAGE. OMG IS THAT DISRESPECTFUL TO TREES?

FIND A WAY
TO TELL A
SECRET ON A
POSTCARD...
REMEMBER THAT
EVERYONE CAN
SEE IT!

THAT WAS AWESOME!

WHAT WAS THAT SONG YOU WERE TELLING ME ABOUT?

WHAT HAVE YOU COLLECTED?
STICKERS? CARDS? SOCK?
LIST OR DRAW BELOW!

Speaking of collecting, there are 8 glasses of water tucked away in this book. Can you find them all? *

THE ONLY THING HERE IS YOU

THINK ON
THE OUTSIDE
OF THE
    SQUARE

(FAMOUS QUOTE)

DRAW SOMETHING
TERRIBLE THAT YOU
CAN'T [UNDO]

IT GETS LONELY SOMETIMES,
BEING A BOOK... IF YOU'VE
EARNED IT, TREAT US BOTH
TO A NEW PEN OR PENCIL!

DRAW BLOOD

(NOT LITERALLY!)

Count from 1 to 100. Now 200. Count until the page is covered! *

leave a big tip!

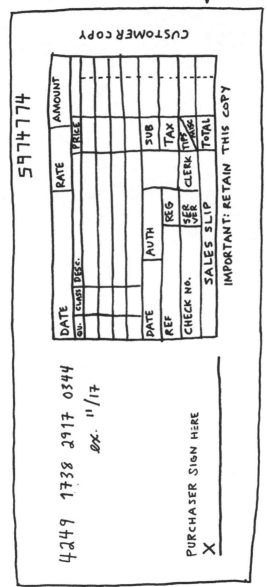

GO TO A PARK.
EWW, NATURE!
DO THEY HAVE WIFI?
DRAW THE BEST TREE.

MAKE A PLAYLIST FOR CRYING:

1. THE ANTLERS
   "I DON'T WANT LOVE"

2.

3.

4.

5.

6.

7.

8.

FILL ALL OF THIS SPACE.
STARE AT IT. NOW MOVE ON.

DRAW OR WRITE "UNDERWATER" BY MAKING EVERYTHING ALL WOBBLY. ADD A FISH, MAYBE.

treat yourself to coffee or tea!

TRY TO START WRITING
SOMETHING BUT NOT
KNOW WHERE IT'S
HEADED OR IF IT'S EVEN
A SENTENCE, BANANA.

SUGGESTED EVENT
GET SOME SUNSHINE
JOIN   MAYBE   HIDE

IT'S JUST PAPER! CUT THIS PAGE INTO A CROWN.

* You might need to cut three strips and do a narrower crown if you have a bigger head! Like if you are a human being, because this is a small book, isn't it.

DECORATE YOUR SPACE WITH THESE PIN-WORTHY RIBBONS!

[📷 SHARE] #JK1PAGE

You DID IT! CONGRATULATIONS!
WRITE A PRESS RELEASE TO
ANNOUNCE YOUR BIG
ACCOMPLISHMENT:

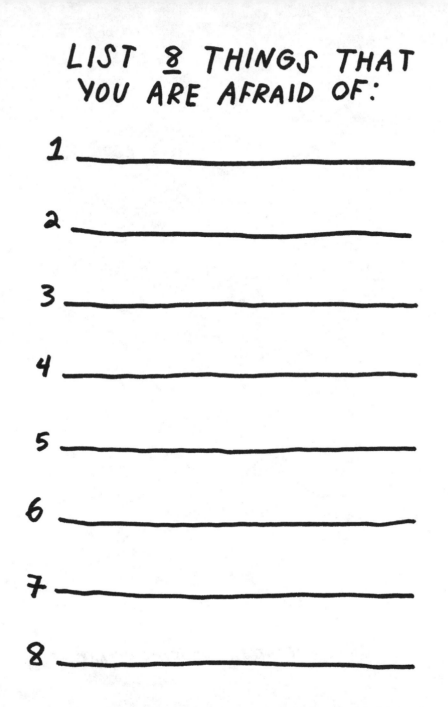

LIST 8 THINGS THAT YOU ARE AFRAID OF:

1 _____

2 _____

3 _____

4 _____

5 _____

6 _____

7 _____

8 _____

* LIFE IS A FULL-TIME JOB

HOW ARE YOU FEELING TODAY?
WHAT IS THE ROOT OF THAT EMOTION?

GIVE THIS PAGE TO A FRIEND

WRITE DOWN A SECRET. GIVE THE
BOOK BACK. DIGEST THE INFORMATION
THEN CROSS IT OUT. NEVER SPEAK OF
THIS EVER AGAIN.

WHAT'S IN YOUR BAG?
DRAW YOUR BAG & ALL
YOUR STUFF!

TAPE AN EMPTY SUGAR
PACKET TO THIS PAGE.
NICE, DUDE, THAT LOOKS SWEET!

WHAT IS
THE POINT
ANYWAY?

HINT

Woah! Bet you didn't realize that this is day 250! What's been your favorite page so far? You've accomplished 249 things already, so pat yourself on the back, and get ready to keep on going. I'm with you to the end! *

WHAT
HAPPENED
LAST
NIGHT?

SOMETIMES DULL,
SOMETIMES SHARP,
ENDLESS POTENTIAL,
BUT NOT PERMANENT
& THAT'S THE POINT.

WRITE IT HUGE

*
SHOUT! SHOUT! SHOUT!

Draw yourself a grid, then check off each box like a tiny accomplishment.
That feels so good! Look how much you've done!

＊

(OMG, I CAN'T BELIEVE
  I PUT THAT IN A BOOK!)

MAYBE YOU SHOULD
HAVE FAITH IN SOMETHING
INTANGIBLE JUST IN CASE.

GO TO THE GROCERY STORE.
WHO DO YOU SEE? SPY ON
THE SHOPPING CARTS.
WHAT DO YOU THINK IS
FOR DINNER? WHO BUYS
THE MOST SNACKS?

MAKE A PLAYLIST FOR TRUE LOVE:

1. LIANNE LA HAVAS
   "EVERYTHING EVERYTHING"

2.

3.

4.

5.

6.

7.

8.

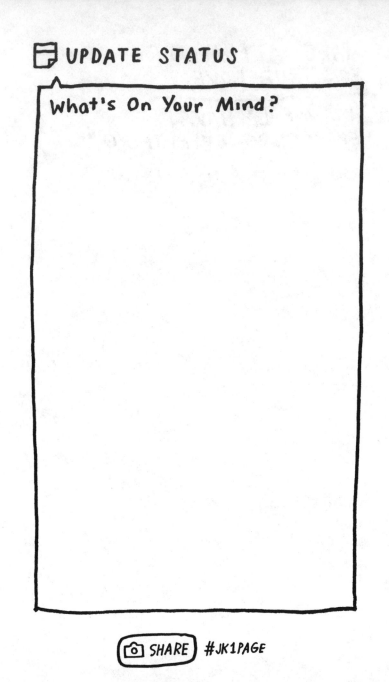

UPDATE STATUS

What's On Your Mind?

SHARE #JK1PAGE

SUMMER CHECKLIST

- ☐ POPSICLE
- ☐ BEACH DAY
- ☐ PICNIC
- ☐ ICE CREAM TRUCK
- ☐ FERRIS WHEEL
- ☐ CORN DOG
- ☐ ROAD TRIP
- ☐ FLIP-FLOPS
- ☐ SHORT HAIR

- ☐ SUN BURN
- ☐ BUG BITE
- ☐ LEMONADE
- ☐ BUTTERFLIES
- ☐ SHORT SHORTS
- ☐ STARRY NIGHTS
- ☐ SUMMER LOVIN'
- ☐ FIREWORKS
- ☐ FLY A KITE

FAVORITES

CIRCLE
ONE

RED BLUE	CHOCOLATE VANILLA	HOT COLD
DAY NIGHT	COFFEE TEA	MOM DAD *JUST KIDDING!* ←
PEN PENCIL	PANTS SHORTS	YESTERDAY TOMORROW
BOYS GIRLS	KETCHUP MUSTARD	CATS DOGS

Sometimes it may seem like there isn't 1 really good choice.
Don't forget, there's always another option. Or change the question! Or don't answer it! You're in control. ✱

✳ Now draw your favorites from the previous page!

WRITE A NOTE TO SOMEONE YOU'VE NEVER MET BEFORE

LAUGHTER IS THE BEST
MEDICINE, BUT YOU KNOW
WHAT ELSE IS? ACTUAL
MEDICINE. IF YOU DON'T
FEEL WELL, GO TO THE
DOCTOR!   FOR NOW,
WRITE DOWN SOME
JOKES FOR THE
WAITING ROOM.

QUARTERLY CHECK-IN

THINK ABOUT THE LAST 3 MONTHS
& RANK YOURSELF ON THE SMILEY SCALE.

LET'S
FACE IT > 😊 😐 ☹️
GOOD FAIR POOR

GENERAL OUTLOOK ◯	PERSONAL GROWTH ◯	PHYSICAL HEALTH ◯
PLANNING AHEAD ◯	TAKING CARE ◯	EATING WELL ◯
SLEEPING HABITS ◯	BEING AWESOME ◯	MENTAL HEALTH ◯
SOME DAILY CREATIVITY ◯	SHOWING KINDNESS ◯	CALLING HOME ◯
WORKING HARD ◯	HAVING FUN ◯	BEING A FRIEND ◯
STAYING CALM ◯	TRYING HARD ◯	ENJOYING YOUR SPACE ◯
EARNING A LIVING ◯	GOING OUTDOORS ◯	THAT 1 THING ◯
FEELING CONTENT ◯	FUNNY TWEETS ◯	FIGURING IT OUT ◯

IT'S JUST PAPER!
FOLD THIS PAGE
IN HALF.

IF YOU HAD TO WEAR THE
SAME OUTFIT EVERY DAY,
WHAT WOULD IT BE? WHAT
IS YOUR ICONIC LOOK?
DESCRIBE OR DRAW BELOW!

FAVORITE BOOKS:

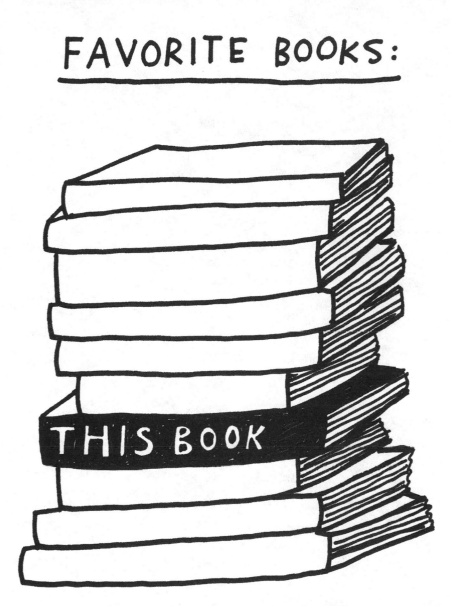

THIS BOOK

(FILL IN THE SPINES!)

DRAW A NEEDLE IN THE
CENTER OF THE PAGE.
NOW DRAW A HAYSTACK.
TRY NOT TO LOSE IT!

THERE IS ALWAYS MORE
(FILL THIS PAGE WITH ASTERISKS)

* * * * * *

HEY, TOUGH GUY!
DRAW SOME T-SHIRTS,
THEN CUT OFF THE SLEEVES.

BEACH DAY! YEEEAAAAHHH! DRAW EVERYTHING YOU NEED:

WHO WAS YOUR CHILDHOOD
BEST FRIEND? HAS THAT
CHANGED? WHERE ARE
THEY NOW?

TAPE A STRAND OF YOUR
HAIR TO THIS PAGE.
1 DAY YOU MIGHT NOT
HAVE ANY LEFT!

*
Remember when you wrote yourself a letter six months ago? Go back and find it!

IT'S JUST PAPER! WRITE "CAUTION" REPEATEDLY, THEN SHRED THE PAGE & THROW IT TO THE WIND.

"This is my throwing page"

*

THIS IS WHAT YOU SAY IT IS

FILL THIS SPACE
WITH BAD HABITS,
THEN CUT IT OUT!

DON'T PAY TOO MUCH ATTENTION
TO OTHER PEOPLE'S CURATED
PUBLIC LIVES. #NOFILTER

WRITE THAT MESSAGE
THAT YOU JUST
CAN'T SEND

LIST 5 PEOPLE YOU USED TO KNOW & WHAT HAPPENED:

1 _____

2 _____

3 _____

4 _____

5 _____

SUGAR
WATER
ZERO DIE
CARAMEL
COLOUR C
12 oz, 355

WRITE A LETTER TO AN
INTERNET "FRIEND" THAT
YOU DON'T KNOW & CAN'T
REMEMBER ADDING.

SEND A PHOTO OF THIS
PAGE AS AN ICEBREAKER.

MAKE A PLAN OF ACTION TO HANDLE YOUR TASKS THIS WEEK:

LOOK UP TODAY! LOOK
FOR BIG CRACKS, CEILING
TILES, & ORNATE DETAILS.
DRAW OR DESCRIBE YOUR
FAVORITE.

MAKE A PLAYLIST FOR SINGING IN THE SHOWER:

1. NATALIE IMBRUGLIA "TORN"

2.

3.

4.

5.

6.

7.

8.

DATE CHECKLIST

- [ ] CHECK HAIR
- [ ] STALK ONLINE
- [ ] 8 PM
- [ ] NEW SHIRT
- [ ] 8:05
- [ ] BREATH MINT
- [ ] THEY'RE HERE!
- [ ] SWEATY PALMS
- [ ] BITE LIP
- [ ] LAUGH LOUD
- [ ] BUTTERFLIES

- [ ] ACT COY
- [ ] MUTUAL FRIEND
- [ ] SMALL TALK
- [ ] LAUGH MORE
- [ ] BIG TALK
- [ ] LET'S DANCE
- [ ] MORE DRINKS
- [ ] FIRST KISS!!
- [ ] MY PLACE?
- [ ] LET'S WAIT
- [ ] TEXT FRIEND

TELL ME ABOUT THAT
REALLY FUNNY THING
THAT HAPPENED:

* Hahaha, oh man. O-K. Whew. Let's take a breather. Tell me something boring while I try to stop giggling.

WOW,
EVERYONE
LOVES YOUR
POST!

 75,631 NOTES

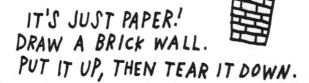

IT'S JUST PAPER!
DRAW A BRICK WALL.
PUT IT UP, THEN TEAR IT DOWN.

If you didn't tear down your wall that is O-K too. Maybe you can let your wall down at your own pace, brick by brick.

*

TELL ME ABOUT YOUR DAY!

WHAT IS THE BEST ADVICE YOU'VE EVER RECEIVED?

WHAT WAS THE FIRST FUNERAL
YOU ATTENDED? DO YOU THINK
IT GETS EASIER? HOW DO YOU
CHERISH & HONOR A LOVED ONE?

LIST 10 THINGS THAT YOU LOVE TO DO:

1 _____

2 _____

3 _____

4 _____

5 _____

6 _____

7 _____

8 _____

9 _____

10 _____

DRAW AN ARM, THEN COVER IT IN TATTOOS!

WE ARE ALL CONNECTED
(FILL THE PAGE WITH WIFI BARS)

BUT WHAT IS THE
Password?

Today is going to be a really good day. ✳

IMAGINE THE COOLEST JOB EVER, THEN DESIGN A BUSINESS CARD FOR YOURSELF!

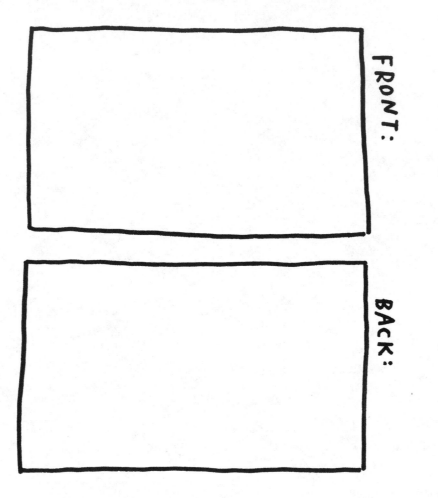

FRONT:

BACK:

WRITE AN EMBARRASSING
STORY ABOUT YOUR BEST
FRIEND SO YOU CAN TELL IT
IN A TOAST AT THEIR WEDDING!

DRAW THE PERFECT MEAL,
THEN COVER IT IN HOT SAUCE!

#JK1PAGE

HEY,

WHERE
ARE
YOU?

WHO WAS THE COOLEST KID
IN SCHOOL? WHERE ARE THEY
NOW? LOOK THEM UP
& SEE HOW THAT GOES.

Go ahead and curse in cursive!
How can something so pretty
be so ~~fucking~~ offensive?

DRAW THE MOST USELESS
THING YOU CAN IMAGINE,
THEN LOVE IT FOREVER.

WRITE IT HUGE

DRAW YOURSELF AS A SPOON.
ARE YOU BIG OR LITTLE?

RUN AWAY FROM IT ALL!
WHERE ARE YOU GOING?
WHAT WILL YOUR NEW NAME BE?

COPY THE LINE 20 TIMES,
OR UNTIL YOU LEARN YOUR LESSON!

I WILL LOOK BACK & LAUGH

TAKE NOTE OF FASHION
TRENDS IN YOUR CITY TODAY.
WHAT DID YOU SEE THE
MOST OF? WHAT WAS UNIQUE?

MAKE A PLAYLIST FOR NOT TALKING:

1. BOARDS OF CANADA "ALPHA AND OMEGA"

2.

3.

4.

5.

6.

7.

8.

TRAVEL PLANS: PLAN AN ALL-AMERICAN ROAD TRIP! WHICH 8 CITIES DO YOU VISIT?

THIS WEEK

- ☐ SLEEP IN
- ☐ FEEL GREAT
- ☐ O-K, KEEP GOING

* treat * yourself to a * night * * out! *

USE THIS PAGE TO PLAN THE
REMAINDER OF YOUR LIFE &
ITS WORK. JUST KIDDING!
WHO'S YOUR CELEB CRUSH?

WHAT'S THE PLAN FOR TODAY?

LOW ON CASH? CUT OUT THE
TEETH BELOW & LEAVE THEM
UNDER YOUR PILLOW!

(DRAW MORE IF YOU NEED THEM)

How is this book almost done? I feel like it's just flown by. Don't leave me! Let's cherish these last pages together.

✳

WAKE UP EARLY TOMORROW TO WATCH
THE SUN RISE. WHO ELSE IS UP?
WHEN WAS THE LAST TIME YOU WERE
UP SO EARLY?

IF SOMEONE HAD NEVER
MET YOU, BUT SEEN YOU
A FEW TIMES, HOW DO
YOU THINK THEY WOULD
DESCRIBE YOU?

LIST 8 PEOPLE YOU WOULD LOVE TO HAVE DINNER WITH:

1 _____

2 _____

3 _____

4 _____

5 _____

6 _____

7 _____

8 _____

READ ANY GOOD BOOKS LATELY?

NO, LIKE WHAT IS THAT BOOK?
YOU THINK ANOTHER BOOK IS
GOING TO TAKE CARE OF YOU
THE WAY I DO? LET ME GUESS,
IT HAS PAGE NUMBERS.

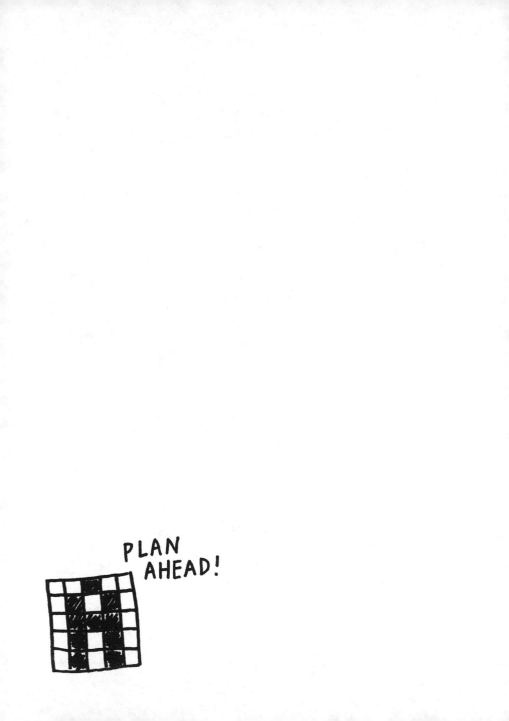

PLAN
AHEAD!

DRAW SIX WATCHES, ONE AT A TIME.

GIVE THIS PAGE TO A FRIEND

SURPRISE ME!

SNEAK A SOUVENIR FROM
A DATE & TAPE IT HERE...
BUT DON'T BE A CREEP!

WRITE SIX SHORT STORIES OF SIX WORDS EACH:

* "This was hard until I finished."

SCRIBBLE
THIS ENTIRE PAGE
WITH ME

Draw a grid. What's the point of it all? I don't know, but try graphing out points and see what you get!

*

THINGS ARE WHAT
YOU MAKE OF THEM...
SO MAKE SOMETHING!

WRITE IT HUGE

*
What do you love about yourself the most?

DOUBLE-TAP

♡

TO LIKE
THIS PAGE

1. DRAW A BICYCLE
2. DRAW A BICYCLE BUILT FOR TWO
3. DRAW A BICYCLE BUILT FOR ZERO

✳ *REMEMBER WHAT IS IMPORTANT TO YOU.*

GO TO THE MALL. BUY NOTHING.
WHAT DID YOU WANT THE MOST?

MAKE A PLAYLIST OF
THE BEST SONG EVER:

1. MARIAH CAREY
   "ALL I WANT FOR
   CHRISTMAS IS YOU"

~~2~~. NO OTHER SONGS

SLOW DOWN

WINTER CHECKLIST

- ☐ SNOW ANGEL
- ☐ HOT COCOA
- ☐ WARM SCARF
- ☐ SPACE HEATER
- ☐ FOGGY GLASSES
- ☐ WHITE BREATH
- ☐ SNOWMAN
- ☐ COLD TOES
- ☐ ICE SKATING
- ☐ SOUP

- ☐ FIREPLACE
- ☐ CUDDLES
- ☐ SKI TRIP
- ☐ ICICLES
- ☐ SHOVEL DUTY
- ☐ IGLOO
- ☐ DIRTY SNOW
- ☐ FEBRUARY
- ☐ WET CLOTHES
- ☐ MORE SOUP

(IT'S OK, I DON'T KNOW WHAT I AM DOING EITHER)

* Sometimes life is difficult and it seems like nothing is working out,
but there's always tomorrow, always another chance. Seriously.

NEVER
FORGET
TO
REMEMBER

IT'S JUST PAPER!
REMEMBER WHEN YOU TAPED
A #5 BILL TO A PAGE?
GO FIND IT & give it away!

QUARTERLY CHECK-IN

THINK ABOUT THE LAST 3 MONTHS
& RANK YOURSELF ON THE SMILEY SCALE.

LET'S
FACE IT 〉   ☺   ☺   ☹
           GOOD   FAIR   POOR

GENERAL OUTLOOK ◯	PERSONAL GROWTH ◯	PHYSICAL HEALTH ◯
PLANNING AHEAD ◯	TAKING CARE ◯	EATING WELL ◯
SLEEPING HABITS ◯	BEING AWESOME ◯	MENTAL HEALTH ◯
SOME DAILY CREATIVITY ◯	SHOWING KINDNESS ◯	CALLING HOME ◯
WORKING HARD ◯	HAVING FUN ◯	BEING A FRIEND ◯
STAYING CALM ◯	TRYING HARD ◯	ENJOYING YOUR SPACE ◯
EARNING A LIVING ◯	GOING OUTDOORS ◯	THAT 1 THING ◯
FEELING CONTENT ◯	FUNNY TWEETS ◯	FIGURING IT OUT ◯

YEARBOOK TIME!
DRAW YOUR HIGH SCHOOL
SELF & GIVE YOURSELF
A SUPERLATIVE.

_____

MOST LIKELY TO:

_____

_____

LIST 5 THINGS THAT YOU WANT TO TRY:

1 _____

2 _____

3 _____

4 _____

5 _____

HOLD YOURSELF
TOGETHER!

YOU MADE IT!

IT'S BEEN A LONG YEAR SINCE YOU FIRST OPENED THIS BOOK, BUT LOOK AT US NOW. YOU'RE 1 YEAR OLDER, AND I'M FULL OF YOUR EXPERIENCES, GOALS AND MORE.

I'M NOT THE SAME AS I WAS. BY DOING 1 PAGE AT A TIME WE HAVE BOTH GROWN. SO GET A PEN & CROSS THAT GUY'S NAME OFF OF THE COVER. YOU DID THIS ON YOUR OWN, & YOU'LL KEEP DOING IT.

CREATE SOMETHING, ANYTHING, EVERY SINGLE DAY. DOCUMENT & SAVE & ADD IT ALL UP. THIS IS YOUR LIFE AND YOU MADE IT.

IT'S JUST PAPER!
TEAR THROUGH THE FINISH LINE.

IT'S JUST PAPER!
TEAR THROUGH THE FINISH LINE.

FILL IN YOUR ACCOMPLISHMENT

WHAT WAS THE MOST
IMPORTANT THING YOU
LEARNED THIS YEAR?

LIST 5 BEST MOMENTS:

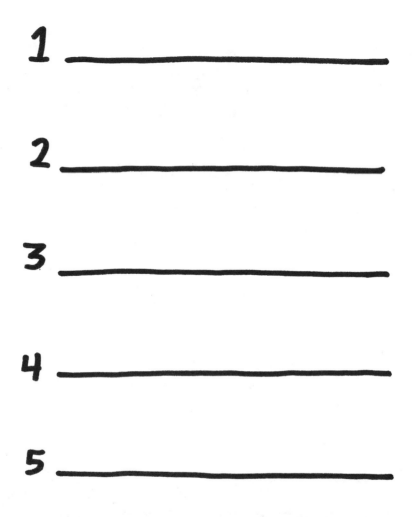

1 _____

2 _____

3 _____

4 _____

5 _____

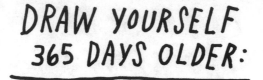

DRAW YOURSELF
365 DAYS OLDER:

WHAT WILL YOU DO NEXT?

#FF @THERESTOFYOURLIFE

FILL THE SPACE WITH SOMETHING GREAT

WHERE YOU'RE GOING

(THIS IS NOT A STEP)

7.

6.

5.

4.

3.

2.

1. SET YOUR GOALS

WHERE YOU ARE

1. THIS WORK IS MY OWN, BUT WOULDN'T BE POSSIBLE WITHOUT A COMMUNITY OF ARTISTS & MAKERS WHOSE LIKE-MINDED CREATIVE WORK IS BOTH INSPIRING & USEFUL.

2. THANK YOU TO EVERYONE WHO BELIEVES IN ME, EVEN WHEN I DON'T KNOW WHAT I'M DOING. I AM GRATEFUL TO ANYONE WHO HAS EVER LOVED A THING I'VE MADE, WRITTEN TO ME, OR PRESSED A HEART-SHAPED BUTTON.

3. I MADE THIS BOOK DURING A DIFFICULT YEAR. IT CAN SEEM IMPOSSIBLE TO GET THROUGH 365 OF ANYTHING, BUT THIS IS MY NOTE TO SELF. THANK YOU TO MY FRIENDS, FAMILY, & MITCHELL KUGA, WHO HAS BEEN BOTH.

4. THANK YOU TO SINGER/SONG-WRITER MICHELLE BRANCH, WHO I DO NOT KNOW PERSONALLY.

ADAM J. KURTZ IS A GRAPHIC DESIGNER, ARTIST, & SERIOUS PERSON. HE IS PRIMARILY CONCERNED WITH CREATING HONEST, ACCESSIBLE WORK, INCLUDING A RANGE OF SMALL PRODUCTS & THE SELF-PUBLISHED "UNSOLICITED ADVICE" CALENDAR SERIES. HE IS THE AUTHOR OF NO OTHER BOOKS, BUT HE'S WORKING ON THAT.

HE CURRENTLY LIVES IN NEW YORK CITY.

VISIT
ADAMJK.COM, @ADAMJK,
& JKJKJKJKJKJKJKJKJK.COM
(OR DON'T!)

✱ Portrait by Ryan Pfluger

Also available from Adam J. Kurtz

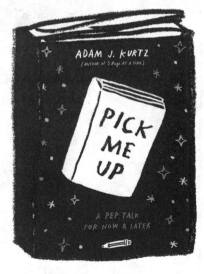